The Cat in the Hat's Learning Library

*To Nancy, Tracie, and all
the monarchs in Mexico, with love.
—T.R.*

The editors would like to thank
BARBARA KIEFER, Ph.D.,
Charlotte S. Huck Professor of Children's Literature,
The Ohio State University, and
DR. DAVID GRIMALDI, Ph.D.,
Curator, Department of Entomology, American Museum of Natural History,
for their assistance in the preparation of this book.

Visit us on the Web!
www.randomhouse.com/kids
Seussville.com

Educators and librarians, for a variety of teaching tools, visit us at www.randomhouse.com/teachers

Library of Congress Cataloging-in-Publication Data
Rabe, Tish.
My, oh my—a butterfly! : all about butterflies / by Tish Rabe ;
illustrated by Aristides Ruiz and Joe Mathieu.
  p. cm. — (The Cat in the Hat's learning library)
Includes index.
ISBN 978-0-375-82882-9 (trade) — ISBN 978-0-375-92882-6 (lib. bdg.)
1. Butterflies—Juvenile literature. I. Ruiz, Aristides, ill. II. Mathieu, Joseph, ill. III. Title. IV. Series.
QL544.2.R33 2007 595.78'9—dc22 2006008371

Printed in the United States of America
22 21 20 19 18 17 16 15 14

My, Oh My— a Butterfly!

by Tish Rabe

illustrated by Aristides Ruiz and Joe Mathieu

The Cat in the Hat's Learning Library®

Random House 🏠 New York

I'm the Cat in the Hat.
If you look in the sky,
you might see a butterfly
fluttering by.

They are colorful insects
whose lives, you will see,
are very exciting.
Come on, follow me!

Right here in your yard,
if you look, you might spot
a butterfly egg.
It's a little round dot.

It sticks to a leaf.

Rain won't wash it away.

Right here on this leaf

is where it wants to stay.

You may think in these eggs

there are small butterflies.

But wait till they hatch

and you'll get a surprise.

Caterpillars hatch out
of a butterfly's eggs!
They look like small worms
and may have sixteen legs.

They start chewing and growing
and growing and chewing,
and that's about all that they
spend their time doing!

They eat first their eggshells.
Then it's leaves that they need.
They eat all the time,
and they grow with great speed.

If we grew as fast as they do—
this was funny to us—
in two weeks, we each would be
as big as a bus!

11

This caterpillar has grown
too big for its skin.
It needs bigger skin than
the skin it's been in.

So it takes a deep breath,
then it wobbles and wiggles.
Its skin starts to split
as it joggles and jiggles.

THIS IS
A SPOT
THAT LOOKS
LIKE AN EYE.

The old skin falls off,
and right there, underneath,
is new, bigger skin
that's been hiding beneath.

12

It eats the old skin.

(Oh, yum! How delicious!)

Protein in the skin

makes it very nutritious.

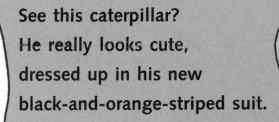

See this caterpillar?
He really looks cute,
dressed up in his new
black-and-orange-striped suit.

After the fourth time
it sheds all its skin,
the next stage of a
butterfly's life will begin.

It hangs upside down
like a small letter "j,"
and for a few hours
it hangs there that way.

14

Then it changes again.
The next stage is this—
a shell forms around it
called a chry-sa-lis.

CHRYSALIS

Inside the chrysalis
the caterpillar *keeps* changing.
All of its body parts
are rearranging.

For almost ten days
it can't move and can't eat.
Then one day
the butterfly's change is complete.

A tiny black leg
begins to poke through.
Within seconds, another
leg pops into view.

She bursts into the air!
A bright new butterfly!
Her wings are so soft
that at first she can't fly.

She must wait till they harden.
Till then, she must stay.
If an enemy comes,
she cannot fly away.

Her antennae start working
to sense what's around her—
the motions, the smells, and
the sights that surround her.

In hours, her new wings
get harder and so

she is ready to fly,
she is ready to go!

See these two caterpillars?
They're different. Here's why—
one will soon be a moth,
one a bright butterfly.

One makes a chrysalis,
and now we know
inside it a butterfly's
starting to grow.

PAINTED LADY
CATERPILLAR

CHRYSALIS

PAINTED LADY
BUTTERFLY

One spins a cocoon
like a blanket to hide it,
and then a new moth begins
growing inside it.

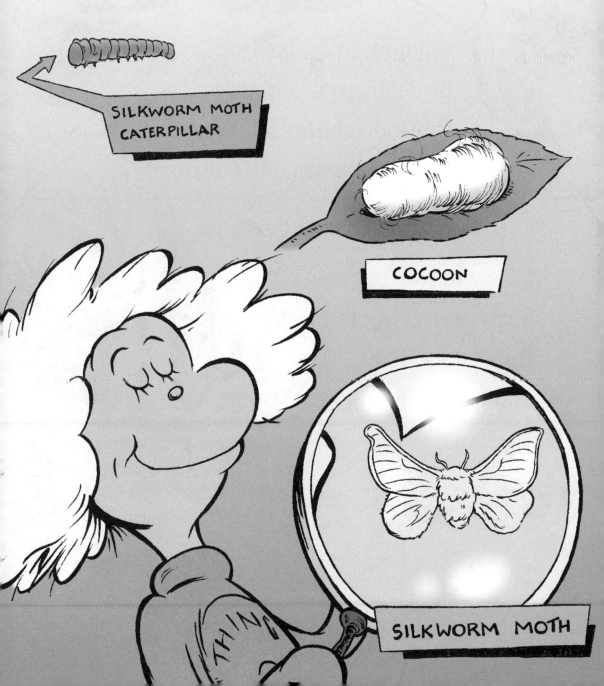

SILKWORM MOTH
CATERPILLAR

COCOON

SILKWORM MOTH

Spiders, frogs, beetles,
birds, lizards, and mice
think bright butterflies
for a snack are quite nice.

Every butterfly knows
birds are trying to catch it.
Its wobbly flight
makes it harder to snatch it!

This butterfly's colors
warn foes it might meet,
"I am poison. I'll hurt you.
I'm NOT good to eat!"
SMALL POSTMAN BUTTERFLY
THING
Some cover their bright wings
with dark wings, you see.
This helps them to blend
with the leaves on a tree.
TOP OF WING
UNDERSIDE
INDIAN LEAF BUTTERFLY

Butterflies are so light.
This will show you how many
you will need just to equal
the weight of a penny.

They see thousands of pictures.
If one looked at me,

here is a drawing
of what it would see.

With this tube, the pro-bos-cis,
a butterfly draws
nectar from flowers
like we drink from straws!

We have a new hobby
we just started trying.
It's fun and it's free,
and it's called butterflying.

We look to find butterflies.
They're everywhere—
in our yard, near a stream,
on the ground, in the air.

PINE WHITE

MOURNING CLOAK

PAINTED LADY

We write down the day
and the time that we saw them.
We write down the place,
then take crayons and draw them.

When you find butterflies,
there are ways you can see
by the size, shape, and color
what kind they might be.

Butterflies get their names
from all different things.
Swallowtail butterflies have
long tails on their wings.

ZEBRA
SWALLOWTAIL

Here is a lacewing.
Its wings look like lace.

This owl butterfly
looks like a baby owl's face.

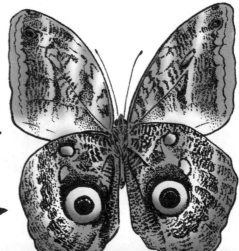

UNDERSIDE OF THE INSECT ▶

Which one is the smallest?
It's this pygmy blue.

A birdwing is largest.
It's beautiful, too!

QUEEN ALEXANDRA'S
BIRDWING

These are the monarchs.
Just watch them in flight!
They have orange and black wings
with small dots of white.

They can't live in cold weather,
so somehow they know
they must fly where it's warmer—
like to Mexico!

They fly hundreds of miles.

They fly hours and hours.

They stop just to rest

and sip nectar from flowers.

Monarchs hide in a storm
when the thunder is crashing.
They know they're in danger
when lightning is flashing.

How do these butterflies know where they're going? Scientists really have no way of knowing!

Butterflies can be tagged to show where they're from. This way we can learn how far they have come.

This one is from Maine, and I think this is cool— it was tagged by the kids at an elementary school!

MAIL TO: BLUE HILL PUBLIC SCHOOL

Monarchs fly for weeks
till they finally see
in the Mexican forest
an oy-a-mel tree.

They fly to the tree,
and then just before dark,
they land and they hook
their small legs in the bark.

Without the sun's warmth
they are too cold for flight,
so they huddle together
to wait out the night.

Blow gently onto
a cold butterfly
and you'll help it warm up
so it's able to fly.

In the spring, when it's warm,
monarchs lift off from the trees.
They flutter and swoop
and they dance in the breeze.

Now that it's warmer,
these butterflies know
they must mate and lay eggs
so new babies can grow.

36

Males look for females
to mate with—it's true—
that have colors and markings
that look like theirs do.

Once a female has mated,
it's hard to go on.
She will not live much longer.
Her time's almost gone.

She is carrying eggs.
They are heavy. That's why
she cannot get back home.
It is too far to fly.

So she searches for leaves
and lays eggs, one by one.
She lays hundreds of eggs
and won't stop till she's done.

Butterflies are surprising
and beautiful things
as they soar through the air
on their bright-colored wings.

They're like jewels in the sun.
They live just a short while,
but whenever you see one
you can't help but smile.

For you know, on a leaf
if you look you may find
an egg that a butterfly
just left behind.

And in this egg—
small as the head of a pin—
a new butterfly life
is about . . .

to begin.

GLOSSARY

Antennae: A pair of long feelers on the head, used to smell and to sense touch.

Chrysalis: A shell that surrounds a grown caterpillar while it changes into a butterfly.

Cocoon: A silky covering that a caterpillar builds around itself before it changes into a moth.

Foe: One who is unfriendly and ready to do harm to another.

Nectar: A sweet liquid found in many flowers.

Nutritious: Providing food necessary for life and growth.

Oyamel: A type of fir tree that grows in the Mexican forests that are the winter home of the monarch butterflies.

Proboscis: A tube-shaped mouth part used for sucking food or drink.

Protein: A substance found in all living things that is necessary to build and sustain them. Eggs, meat, fish, and beans are good sources of protein.

FOR FURTHER READING

Butterflies and Moths by Paul A. Opler, illustrated by Amy Bartlett Wright (Houghton Mifflin, *Peterson First Guides*). A relatively simple field guide for beginning naturalists. Includes the most common butterflies and moths in North America. For grades 3 and up.

The Butterfly Alphabet by Kjell B. Sandved (Scholastic). Truly amazing photographs show the letters of the alphabet as seen on butterfly wings! For kindergarten and up.

Hurry and the Monarch by Antoine Ó Flatharta, illustrated by Meilo So (Alfred A. Knopf Books for Young Readers). A beautifully illustrated story about a migrating monarch butterfly who stops to rest on the back of a Texas tortoise named Hurry. Includes an afterword about monarch migration. For kindergarten and up.

Where Did the Butterfly Get Its Name? Questions and Answers About Butterflies and Moths by Melvin and Gilda Berger, illustrated by Higgins Bond (Scholastic). All about butterflies and moths. For grades 3 and up.

INDEX